AMERICAN CIRCUS POSTERS

IN FULL COLOR

edited by
CHARLES PHILIP FOX

Dover Publications, Inc.
New York

Introduction

Literally, the traveling tented circus was "here today—gone tomorrow."

Since the show would usually be in town for only one day, and give only two performances, the circus management contrived ahead of time many ways to advertise.

Approximately two weeks prior to show day, the advance crew of the circus arranged for the publication of advertisements in newspapers, the distribution of heralds and the mailing of couriers to let everyone know their show was coming to town.

The most important tool used by the advertising crew was the lithograph or poster.

Posters of ½-sheet size or 1-sheet size (28″ x 42″) were hung in store windows by the hundreds. Posters of larger sizes, such as 3-sheet (42″ x 84″), 6-, 9-, 16-, 20-, 28-sheet and many other sizes, including, rarely, 100-sheets, were pasted on sheds, barns, buildings, walls and fences. When appropriate space was not available, the billposters simply went to the local lumberyard, purchased the necessary material, built a board fence around a vacant lot, and then pasted their posters on it.

The circus poster was used profusely. The big railroad circuses thought nothing of using 5,000 to 8,000 sheets per town. If competition from another circus showed up, the quantity of paper used might easily double.

The fifty-year period between 1880 and 1930 was what might be called the great days of the circus poster. There were dozens of lithograph houses that turned out handsome work. Among the leaders were the Strobridge and Enquirer Companies of Cincinnati; Donaldson of Newport, Kentucky; Riverside of Milwaukee; Erie of Erie, Pennsylvania; and Courier of Buffalo.

The circus, of course, was a subject that was colorful and exciting and it was easy for the lithographers to produce designs loaded with action and all the colors of the rainbow.

The magnificence of their work—from artist to platemaker to pressman—is exemplified in the representative posters reproduced in this book.

The posters were scrutinized from sidewalks, from horseback, from wagons or carriages and later from streetcars and autos. The detail was exquisite whether they were viewed from five feet or 50 feet away.

The color and artwork instantly caught the eye. Perhaps the subject was a beautiful, lithe lady on a prancing white horse. Perhaps a startling tiger would be charging right at you, or perhaps it was the graceful aerial acts that attracted attention. These and hundreds of other designs ingrained in the public's mind the fact that the circus was coming.

On every poster the name or title of the circus was clearly printed. Alongside the posters were conspicuous date sheets that told the name of the show town, the day of the week, the date and the month. Repetition of these facts, "Madison, Tuesday, May 27" would subconsciously sink into the viewer's mind.

The reason for showing the name of the town was simple. Circus billers would post towns 15 and 20 miles out (and more) in all directions from the community where the circus would put up its tents.

All of this advertising, as we have seen, was handled by a crew who traveled in advance of the show.

If it was a small wagon circus, the advance crew likewise traveled in horse-drawn vehicles and stayed in town only one day so they could keep two weeks ahead of the show.

Railroad circuses used railroad cars to carry their advance crews. Depending on the size of the circus, they used from one to four cars, each with a crew of from 20 to 30 men.

The first car would arrive in town about two weeks before the show, the second a few days later, and the second crew would cover additional territory.

The men of the advance knew that their advertising had to do a job because the circus they worked for would generally be in town for such a brief time. Nothing was left to chance and they saw to it that this wonderful and colorful and exciting paper was put up in every feasible spot.

The lithographers gave them the best possible tools—their posters. The advance crew got them up where they could be seen. On circus day, when people crowded out to the showgrounds, jammed up in front of the ticket wagons and shoved the shekels of the realm onto the counter, receiving in return a small piece of paper called a ticket—then and then only did everyone know the beautiful posters had done the job for which they were designed.

CHARLES PHILIP FOX

Published in Canada by General Publishing Company, Ltd., 30 Lesmill Road, Don Mills, Toronto, Ontario.

Published in the United Kingdom by Constable and Company, Ltd., 10 Orange Street, London WC2H 7EG.

American Circus Posters in Full Color is a new work, first published by Dover Publications, Inc., in 1978.

International Standard Book Number: 0-486-23693-5
Library of Congress Catalog Card Number: 78-54311

Manufactured in the United States of America
Dover Publications, Inc.
180 Varick Street
New York, N.Y. 10014

Notes on the Plates

The numbers are those of the pages on which the posters are illustrated.

Front cover: May Wirth, superstar of the 1910s and 1920s, captured the hearts of all who witnessed her act. This attractive girl from Australia, who always wore a large bow in her hair, performed incredible bareback-riding feats.

Inside front cover: In the winter of 1918/1919 the Ringling Bros., who since 1907 had owned the Barnum & Bailey circus as well as their own, decided to combine the two shows into one gigantic aggregation. Always frugal, they did not scrap their inventory of posters advertising Barnum & Bailey alone, but instructed their printers, the celebrated Strobridge Lithographing Company of Cincinnati, to devise ways of using this obsolete stock. Under the Barnum & Bailey banner, the present poster had advertised the menagerie (note the copyright date of 1916). Strobridge printed and hand-pasted a sticker that referred to Ringling Bros., covering over the reference to the menagerie. Thus we have what is probably the only circus poster on which the famous title of the combined shows is reversed.

Inside back cover: In this 1912 poster, the Strobridge artists cleverly separated the six scenes by means of outlines and balanced color areas, creating a fascinating composite of the various routines one would expect to see at the circus performance.

Back cover: The Sparks Circus, which moved on 20 railroad cars, was always well received. The show was large enough to order special paper depicting certain acts. Mixed animal presentations were always popular. This poster, by the Erie Lithograph Co. of Erie, Pa., dates from the 1920s.

1: All big circuses in the first half of the twentieth century carried a large menagerie of wild animals. This was a popular and highly educational feature. The attractive montage on this Erie Lithograph poster of the 1920s indicates the vast and varied collection of animals that would be on display.

2: In the days of the big tented circuses, the hippodrome races, usually reserved for the finale, were especially exciting. The furiously thundering hooves of the galloping horses would bring the entire audience to their feet. This is a Strobridge poster of the 1890s.

3: No doubt at least three artists worked on a poster like this 1906 Strobridge example. One man might be adept at drawing horses, another very good with the human figure and a third clever with lettering or design. This combination of efforts was one of the reasons the artwork was rarely signed.

4: In 1904, as this Strobridge poster shows, the Clarkonians performed what is known as the "double double"—two somersaults and two pirouettes before being caught. The Flying Gaonas do this act today on the "Greatest Show on Earth."

5: On this Strobridge poster, the press agents of 1905 called this thrill act "a fearful frolic with fate." Indeed, all acts of this type—whether the performers operated somersaulting autos, rode hurtling bicycles over enormous gaps, or were catapulted from a huge crossbow or shot out of a cannon—were truly daring and dangerous.

6: This Strobridge poster of 1909 has an extremely graceful flow of line and unusually subtle color effects and relationships.

7: In 1909 Desperado made his "terrific descent" twice a day, and sometimes three times. The Strobridge artists captured all of the thrill of this unbelievable act.

8: In this poster of the 1920s the artist has made a clever composite of the routines performed by these male lions. In actuality, the trainer would put these big cats through their paces one trick at a time; this avoids confusion and keeps each animal's attention riveted on the particular routine for which he is responsible.

9: Tiger acts have always been popular because of the enormous size of the animals and their startling beauty. The black leopard was added to the group for variety and perhaps for prestige. This poster dates back to the 1920s, when there were some 50 men and women trainers presenting big-cat acts on 14 circuses.

10: In 1903 Barnum & Bailey presented an unusually lavish Spectacle of Balkis (the Arabic name of the biblical Queen of Sheba). At this period all the big railroad circuses staged these pantomine productions involving hundreds of beautifully wardrobed people, scores of horses and dozens of elephants, camels, zebras and llamas. The subject might be Joan of Arc, Cinderella or Nero and the Burning of Rome. All these productions were part of the circus, presented in the big tent. Strobridge poster.

11: Both the artwork and the insistent text of this Strobridge poster of 1896 emphasize the bigness of the show. The thousands of circus-bound people pouring out of the excursion trains clinch the effect.

12: Although the daily street parade was in itself an advertisement that let the townspeople know for sure that it was circus day, the big shows used posters that advertised the advertisement! Strobridge poster, 1912.

13: Only a circus could promise, all on one poster, a Moorish Caravan, a Roman Hippodrome and an Imperial Japanese Troupe. All this conjured up the intrigue, pomp and astounding tricks that would be seen at the big show. Strobridge poster, 1893.

14: Seven scenes of beautiful horses and handsomely attired performers, neatly put together on one 1906 poster by the Strobridge artists, tell the whole story at a glance.

15: The wreath effectively sets off the formal group portrait of the equestrian family, and the shield below adds impact to their name. The scenes of the family in action are so vivid that only 12 words are needed to describe the act. Strobridge poster, 1909.

16: Barnum & Bailey played the entire season of 1902 in France. For this tour, posters like this Strobridge one were printed in America and shipped to the circus advertising department in France. Translation of the text: "For the children: all kinds of tricks by trained animals. The largest and most wonderful entertainment organization in the world."

17: To illustrate bears wire walking, stilt walking, riding bicycles, skating, dancing and playing instruments all on one poster is not an easy task. But the artists of this sheet from the 1920s accomplished the feat of an unconfused arrangement. The result makes you want to see the bears actually perform.

18: This poster, which embodies three main elements of the circus—beautiful girls, clowns and animals—was designed to announce the historic union of the Ringling Bros. circus with that of Barnum & Bailey in the winter of 1918/1919.

19: Designed by the Norman Bel Geddes Studio in the 1940s, this poster with the snarling leopard has set some kind of record for length of service, since—with changes in lettering style over the years—it was still in use in the 1970s.

20: The slogans "100 Clowns—Count 'Em—100" and "An Army of Clowns," as on this poster of the 1920s, were commonly used to emphasize an important facet of any circus performance.
21: Five of the midget bareback rider's tricks are shown on this one 1915 Strobridge poster, and only a few words of explanatory text are required.
22: When this Strobridge poster was designed in 1914, traffic and life in general moved at a slower pace than today. There was time to study the detail that the lithograph artists worked into their product. Twenty-two Chinese performers and three standard-bearers are woven into this composite drawing.
23: Pageantry, excitement and color are skillfully blended in this poster from the 1920s. If you went to this show you would see all these ingredients, but not simultaneously. While the parade on the hippodrome track was being presented, no acts would be taking place. If bareback acts were going on, there would be no aerial acts at the same time.
24: Beautiful girls, stunning wardrobe, magnificent horses, a charming trainer, a clown, ring curbs and props—all these put together in one scene result in an extremely attractive circus poster. From the 1920s.
25: This identical design, only with the horses pure white, was used during the 1910s by the Ringling Bros. World's Greatest Shows. A decade later, when the circus had a liberty act of bay horses (in a liberty act, the horses perform freely in the ring without lines or riders), an artist simply changed the color of the horses to conform with the current attraction.
26: The six smaller panels with elephant routines, barring slight variations in scale, are true to life, but the central illustration can only be attributed to artistic license. When attending the show, however, the average spectator felt that all the elephants were enormous, and it never entered his head to compare the poster art with what he actually witnessed.
27: This poster of the 1900 era, by the Courier Lithograph Company of Buffalo, N.Y., calls the menagerie an "Exposition of Natural History," and it was a truly educational adjunct to the circus. Audiences of the hinterland were especially fascinated by the exotic beasts which they had never seen before.
28: To emphasize the marble-statue appearance of the two performers, the artists used a black background, although black was a color rarely found to any great extent on circus posters. Strobridge poster, 1890s.
29: This highly animated poster gains additional interest from the female driver of the foreground quadriga. From the 1930s.
30: Posters devoted to a single clown act were not at all common. These seven scenes introduce an outstanding team of the day. A neat little touch shows Carroll in makeup painting his own portrait. Strobridge poster, 1893.
31: Although the nursery-rhyme floats are the center of interest in this Strobridge poster of 1893, the artists also included a broadside view of the main tent. This added feature immediately indicates that this circus is a big one.
32: Fine horses are among the mainstays of any circus. To promenade the prancing beauties in one huge column around the hippodrome track created a great spectacle. The artists of this 1897 Strobridge poster caught all of the feel of this grand march.

33: Ethnological exhibits showing the customs of exotic nations—dances, instruments, attire and dwellings—were sometimes part of the educational display in the menagerie tents of the big railroad circuses. Strobridge poster, 1894.

34: Even circus elephants became involved in this pageant of Aladdin and his lamp. The colorfully dressed participants, majestic horse-drawn floats and richly caparisoned horses fill this glorious Strobridge poster of 1917.

35: The elephants' robes, the horses' trappings, the costumes, flags, banners, howdahs and throne all contribute to the sumptuous and colorful splendor of the 1916 Strobridge poster.

36: Gargantua was the most heavily billed and promoted circus attraction since Barnum's elephant Jumbo in the early 1880s. From 1938, the date of this Strobridge poster, through 1948, Gargantua traveled from one end of the United States to the other in a huge air-conditioned cage.

37: Giraffes were rare zoological features and the inhabitants of the hinterland gazed with awe on these almost incredible creatures. Strobridge poster, 1917.

38: Poster artists were called upon to portray acts and routines exactly as they were performed. An intricate presentation like this one demanded all the dexterity and talent an artist could muster. The result is a true-to-life rendition of a complicated, seemingly entangled situation. Strobridge poster, 1903.

39: To fully appreciate the complex routines of this "equestrian sensation," the viewer must stop and study the artwork. The course of the flying, somersaulting bodies is shown with dotted lines and arrows. The sudden appearance of a 24-sheet version of this poster on some old, weatherbeaten fence was sure to attract attention in any town. Strobridge poster, 1913.

40: Portraits of the owners were used profusely on circus posters to give the townspeople a feeling of confidence in the show they were about to see. Strobridge poster, 1890s.

41: Only three men, not 13, were in this troupe. The artists' purpose was not to deceive but only to show the various routines that the Herbert Brothers could accomplish. Strobridge poster, 1890s.

42: Trained pigs were frequently seen on the traveling circuses. An act of trained house cats might have been included more often on the tiny dog and pony shows, but the one illustrated in this poster of a huge railroad circus is indeed a rarity. Strobridge poster, 1890s.

43: Rarely were posters devoted to snakes. The reptiles did not "act" in the true sense of the word; their one desire was to slither out of the grasp of the "snake charmer" and get back to more comfortable surroundings. In the process, viewers were fascinated by the gliding of the creatures. Strobridge poster, 1894.

44: The brilliant red carpet laid on the performing platform sets off the seals and, of course, quickly attracts the eye. The descriptive copy is typical of the boastful way the circus had of proclaiming its acts as something very special. From the 1930s.

The author thanks Ringling Bros. and Barnum & Bailey Combined Shows, Inc. for permission to reproduce in this book advertising material involving circus names they own. These names are:

Ringling Bros. and Barnum & Bailey Circus
Barnum & Bailey Greatest Show on Earth
Ringling Bros. World's Greatest Shows
Sells-Floto Circus
Hagenbeck-Wallace Circus
Sparks Circus
Al G. Barnes Circus
Forepaugh-Sells Bros. Circus
John Robinson Circus

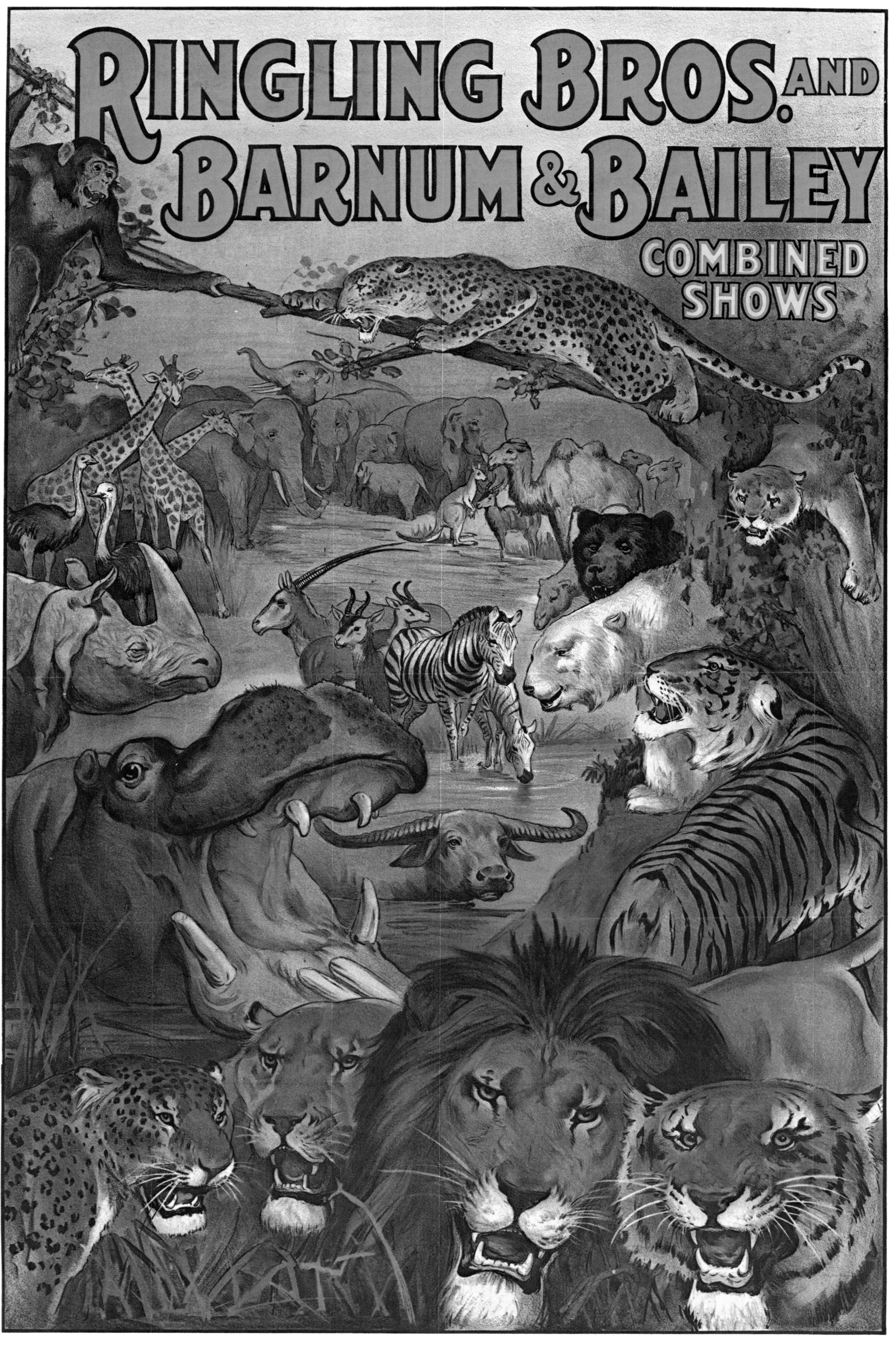
RINGLING BROS. AND
BARNUM & BAILEY
COMBINED
SHOWS

·SELLS·BROTHERS'·ENORMOUS·UNITED·SHOWS·
INTERIOR SCENE GIVING AN EXACT REPRESENTATION OF THE MANY ACTS IN TWO RINGS, MID-AIR, ELEVATED STAGE AND HIPPODROME, EVERY ACT HEREIN PICTURED, MOST POSITIVELY SEEN AT EACH EXHIBITION TOGETHER WITH FIFTY MORE
THE STROBRIDGE LITH Co CIN'TI NY LONDON
REAL ROMAN HIPPODROME
THREE RING CIRCUS
· ELEVATED STAGE ·
FIVE CONTINENT MENAGERIE

THE BARNUM & BAILEY
GREATEST SHOW ON EARTH
BRADNA & DERRICK
CHAMPION PRINCIPAL & TRICK RIDERS OF THE WORLD
EN ROUTE TO THE RACES OR A COACHING PARTY ON A LARK
LES ROWLANDES. A DOZEN FEARLESS FRENCH RIDERS IN A WILD EQUESTRO COACHING SATURNALIA.
THE RIDING ROONEYS
IN A SERIES OF MOST REMARKABLE EQUESTRIAN EXPLOITS.

THE BARNUM & BAILEY
GREATEST SHOW ON EARTH
1
2
3
THE MARVELOUS MID-AIR PIROUETTE OR
"TWISTING DOUBLE SOMERSAULT"
A FEAT NEVER BEFORE ATTEMPTED
BY THE MOST INTREPID AERIALISTS
"WATCH THEM"
THE ASTOUNDING CLARKONIANS
COPYRIGHT 1904 BY
THE STROBRIDGE LITHO CO.
CINCINNATI & NEW YORK

THE BARNUM & BAILEY
GREATEST SHOW ON EARTH
M'LLE MAURICIA DE TIERS
L'AUTO BOLIDE THRILLING DIP OF DEATH
M'LLE MAURICIA DE TIERS, THE FEARLESS, YOUNG AND FASCINATING
PARISIAN, IN A DREADFUL, HEADLONG LEAP, LOOP AND TOPSY TURVY PLUNGING SOMERSAULT WITH AN AUTOMOBILE
THE SENSATION OF ALL SENSATIONS, WHICH MAY BE APTLY TERMED A FEARFUL FROLIC WITH FATE
AN ABSOLUTELY UNPARALLELED DEED OF DARING, JUST AS ILLUSTRATED AND COSTING NEARLY $2000.00 A MINUTE
THE MOST EXPENSIVE, AS WELL AS THE MOST HAZARDOUS ACT EVER DEVISED.
COPYRIGHT 1905 BY THE STROBRIDGE LITHO. CO. CIN'TI & NEW YORK.

THE BARNUM & BAILEY
LATEST AND GREATEST
THRILLER
THE BALLOON HORSE
JUPITER
in his
Sensational Ascension Act
with a gorgeous
Pyrotechnic Display
AT
EVERY PERFORMANCE
OF
THE GREATEST SHOW ON EARTH
COPYRIGHT 1909 BY
THE STROBRIDGE LITHO. CO.
CINCINNATI & NEW YORK

THE BARNUM & BAILEY

GREATEST SHOW ON EARTH

THE THRILLER SUPREME

DESPERADO'S

TERRIBLE LEAP FOR LIFE

A TERRIFIC DESCENT OF 80 FEET

THROUGH SPACE

LANDING UPON HIS CHEST

ON A SKID

PLACED AT AN ANGLE

OF 50 DEGREES

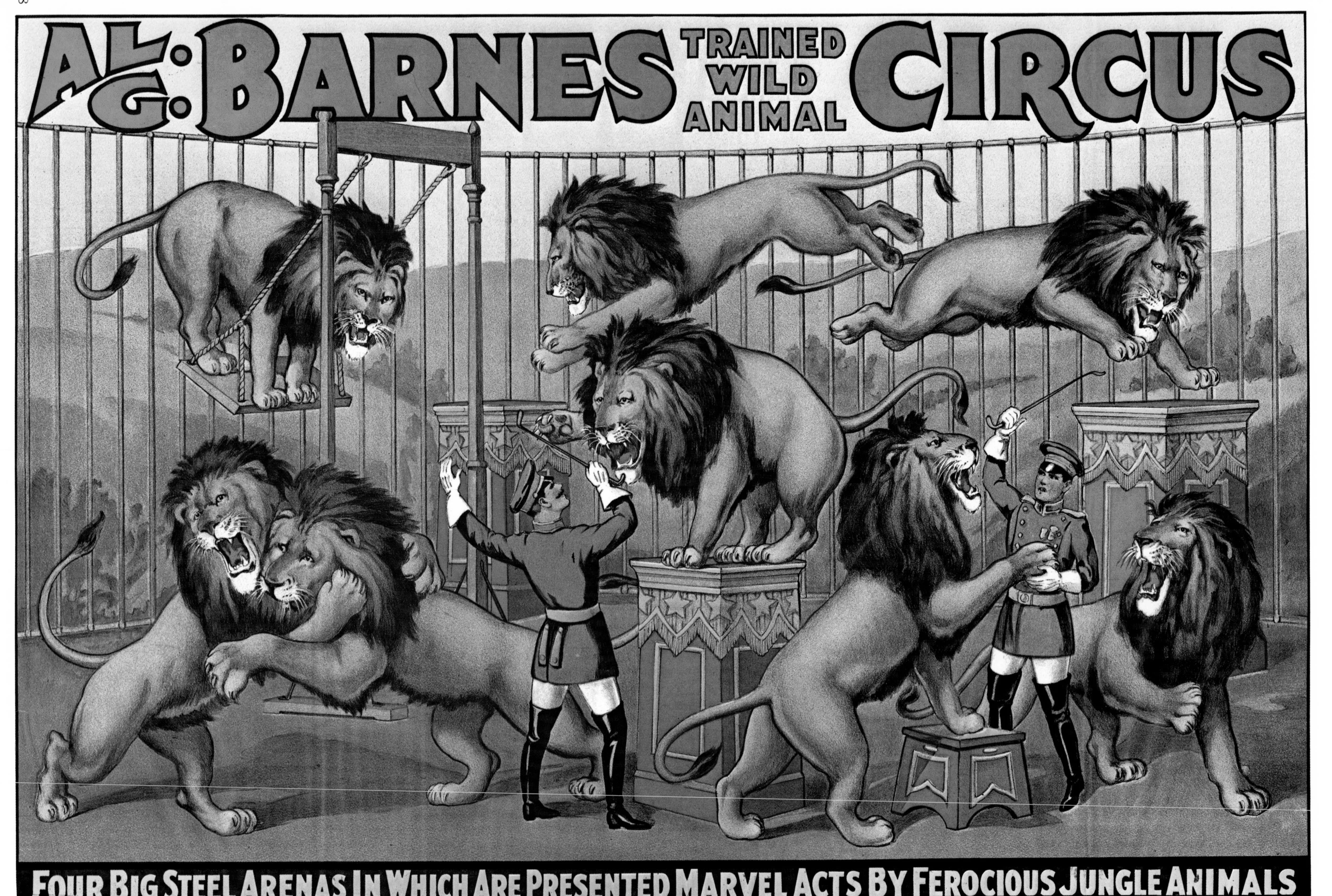
Al. G. Barnes
Trained Wild Animal
Circus
Four Big Steel Arenas In Which Are Presented Marvel Acts By Ferocious Jungle Animals

RINGLING BROS AND BARNUM & BAILEY
COMBINED SHOWS
THE GREATEST SHOW ON EARTH
NEW JUNGLE CIRCUS
A COMPLETE BIG TRAINED ANIMAL SHOW GRATUITOUSLY ADDED

The Barnum & Bailey Greatest Show on Earth
THE SPECTACLE OF BALKIS – A VERITABLE VISION OF ANCIENT GLORIES, MARCHES, TABLEAUX, DANCING GIRLS, MOUNTED GUARDS AND TRULY LAVISH DISPLAYS OF COSTUMES, ANIMATED LIFE AND COLOR.
THE WORLD'S LARGEST, GRANDEST, BEST, AMUSEMENT INSTITUTION.

FOREPAUGH & SELLS BROTHERS GREAT SHOWS CONSOLIDATED
AMERICA'S GREATEST SHOWS
IN MIGHTY UNION
THE ADAM FOREPAUGH GREAT SHOW
SELLS BROTHERS BIG SHOW OF THE WORLD
EXCURSIONS FROM ALL POINTS
THE GREAT ADAM FOREPAUGH SHOW COMBINED WITH SELLS BROTHERS BIG SHOW OF THE WORLD
CENTRAL R. R.
TO THE ADAM FOREPAUGH & SELLS BROTHERS GR
THE MOST STUPENDOUS MENAGERIE, CIRCUS, HIPPODROME ANNEX HORSE AND HOTEL TENTS EVER KNOWN.

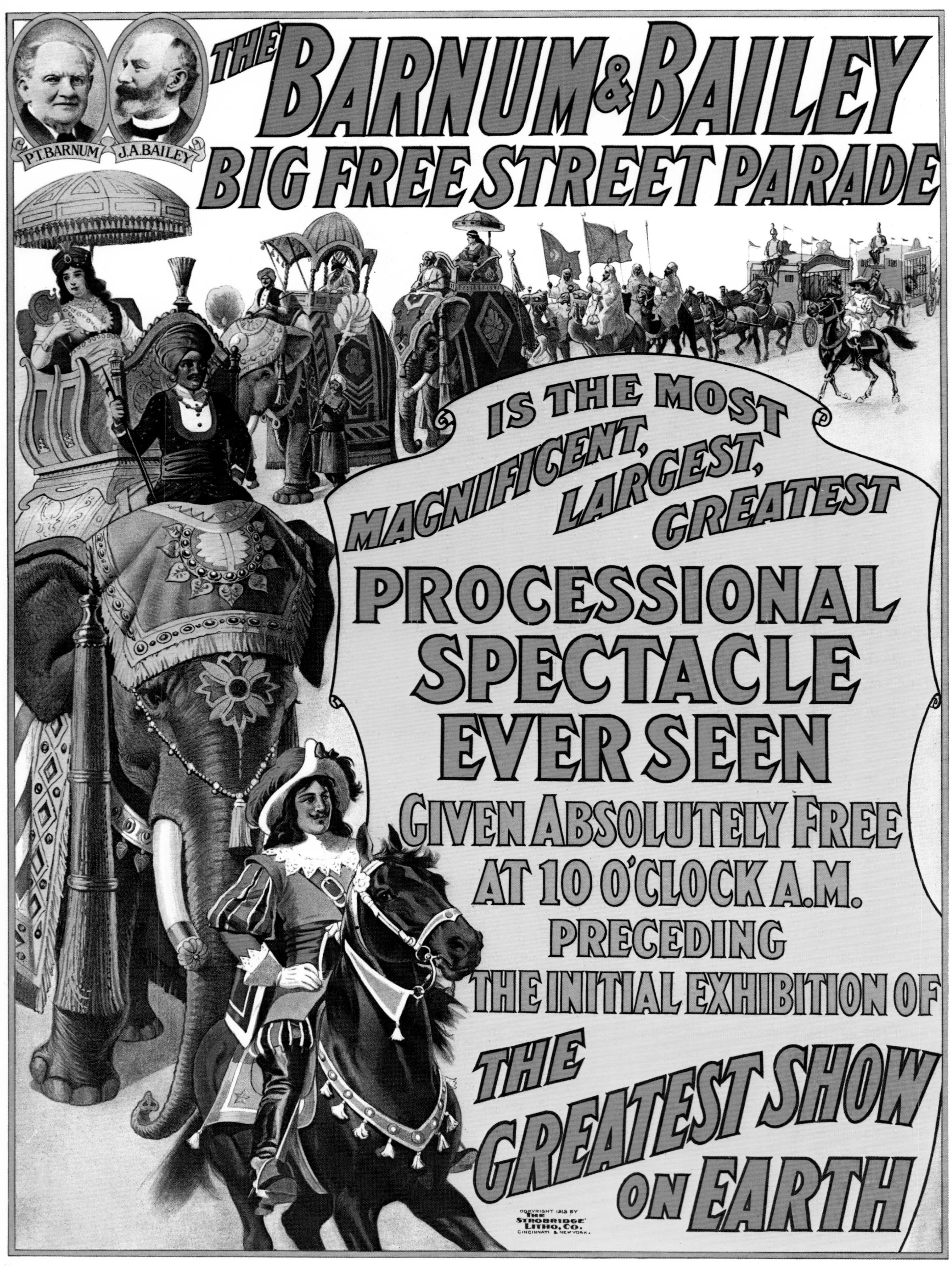
P.T. BARNUM
J.A. BAILEY
THE BARNUM & BAILEY
BIG FREE STREET PARADE
IS THE MOST
MAGNIFICENT,
LARGEST,
GREATEST
PROCESSIONAL
SPECTACLE
EVER SEEN
GIVEN ABSOLUTELY FREE
AT 10 O'CLOCK A.M.
PRECEDING
THE INITIAL EXHIBITION OF
THE
GREATEST SHOW
ON EARTH
COPYRIGHT 1912 BY
THE
STROBRIDGE
LITHO, CO.
CINCINNATI & NEW YORK.

ROMAN HIPPODROME
3 RING CIRCUS
TWO ELEVATED STAGES,
5 CONTINENT MENAGERIE
IMPERIAL JAPANESE TROUPE
SELLS BROTHERS
COMBINED WITH
HASSAN BEN ALI'S
MOORISH CARAVAN
ARABIAN NIGHTS' ENTERTAINMENT
AND SPECTACULAR
PILGRIMAGE TO MECCA
20 YEARS BEFORE THE PUBLIC.
THE SUPREME TEST OF MERIT IS SUCCESS.
ORIENTALLY SPLENDID AND WEIRDLY ROMANTIC SPECTACULAR PILGRIMAGE TO MECCA.
INTRODUCING THE ONLY BERBER AND BEDOUIN TRIBAL CARAVAN OF MOORISH BARBARIANS AND WARRIORS.
THE STROBRIDGE LITH. CO.

THE BARNUM & BAILEY
GREATEST SHOW ON EARTH
A WHOLE HORSE SHOW
OF THE MOST PERFECTLY TRAINED THOROUGHBRED HIGH SCHOOL HORSES IN THE WORLD
IN A MOST MARVELOUS DISPLAY OF GRACEFUL, DIFFICULT AND DASHING EQUESTRIANISM.

THE BARNUM & BAILEY
GREATEST SHOW ON EARTH
THE GREAT HUNGARIAN RIDERS
THE KÖNYÖT FAMILY
COPYRIGHT 1909 BY THE STROBRIDGE LITHO CO CINCINNATI & NEW YORK
ABSOLUTELY THE WORLD'S FOREMOST EQUESTRIANS

The Barnum & Bailey Greatest Show on Earth
POUR LES ENFANTS: TOURS DE TOUTES SORTES PAR DES ANIMAUX SAVANTS.
PRINTED IN AMERICA.
L'INSTITUT DE DIVERTISSEMENT LE PLUS GRAND ET LE PLUS MAGNIFIQUE DU MONDE.

RINGLING BROS
AND
BARNUM & BAILEY
COMBINED SHOWS
PALLENBERG'S Wonder BEARS
BRUINS THAT DANCE, SKATE, WALK TIGHT ROPES and RIDE BICYCLES LIKE HUMANS

RINGLING
BROS
AND
BARNUM
& BAILEY
A
COLOSSAL
COMBINATION
OF
ALL
THAT IS
GREAT
IN
CIRCUS
ACHIEVEMENT

Ringling Bros.
AND
Barnum & Bailey
GH
CIRCUS
THE GREATEST SHOW ON EARTH

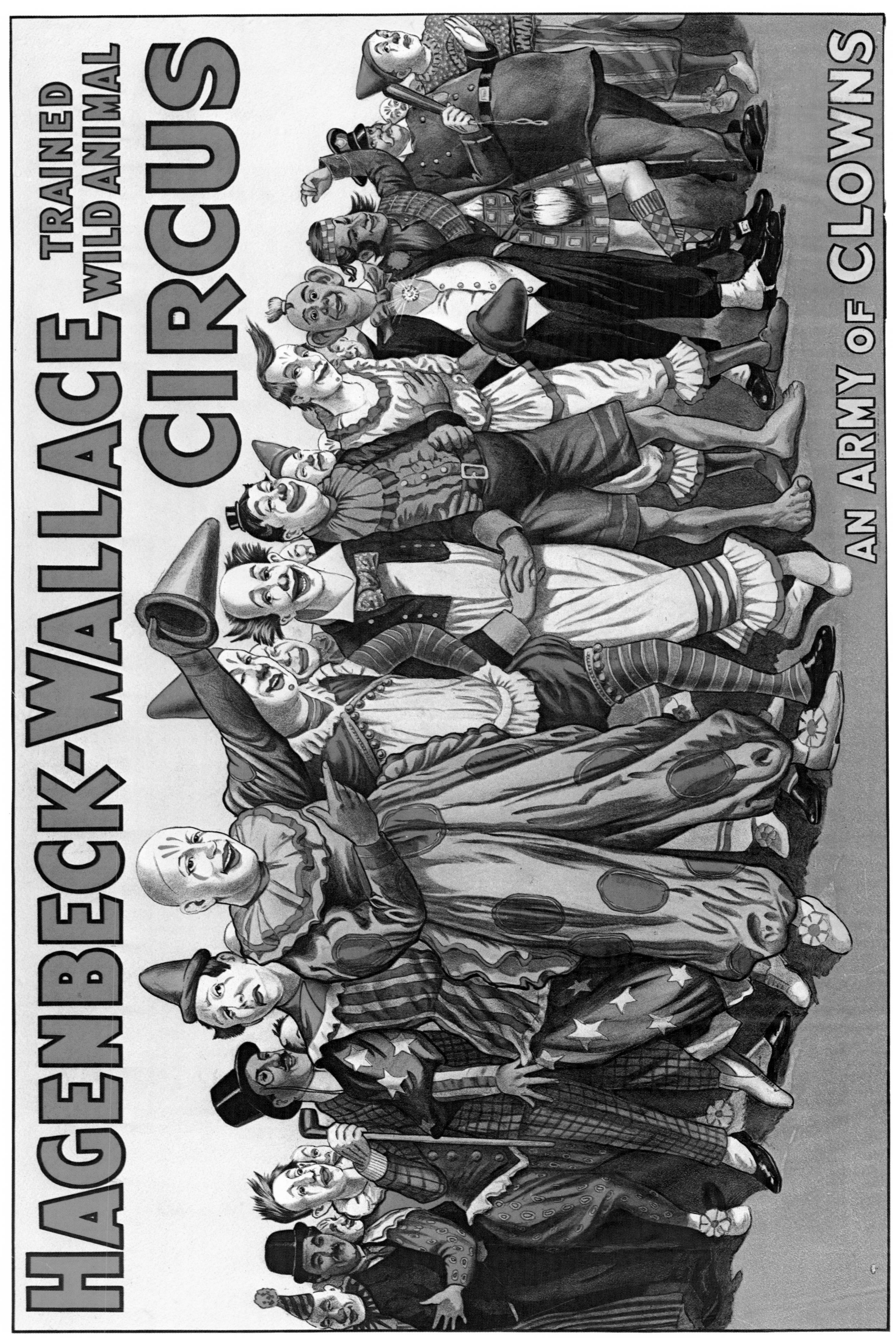
HAGENBECK-WALLACE
TRAINED
WILD ANIMAL
CIRCUS
AN ARMY OF CLOWNS

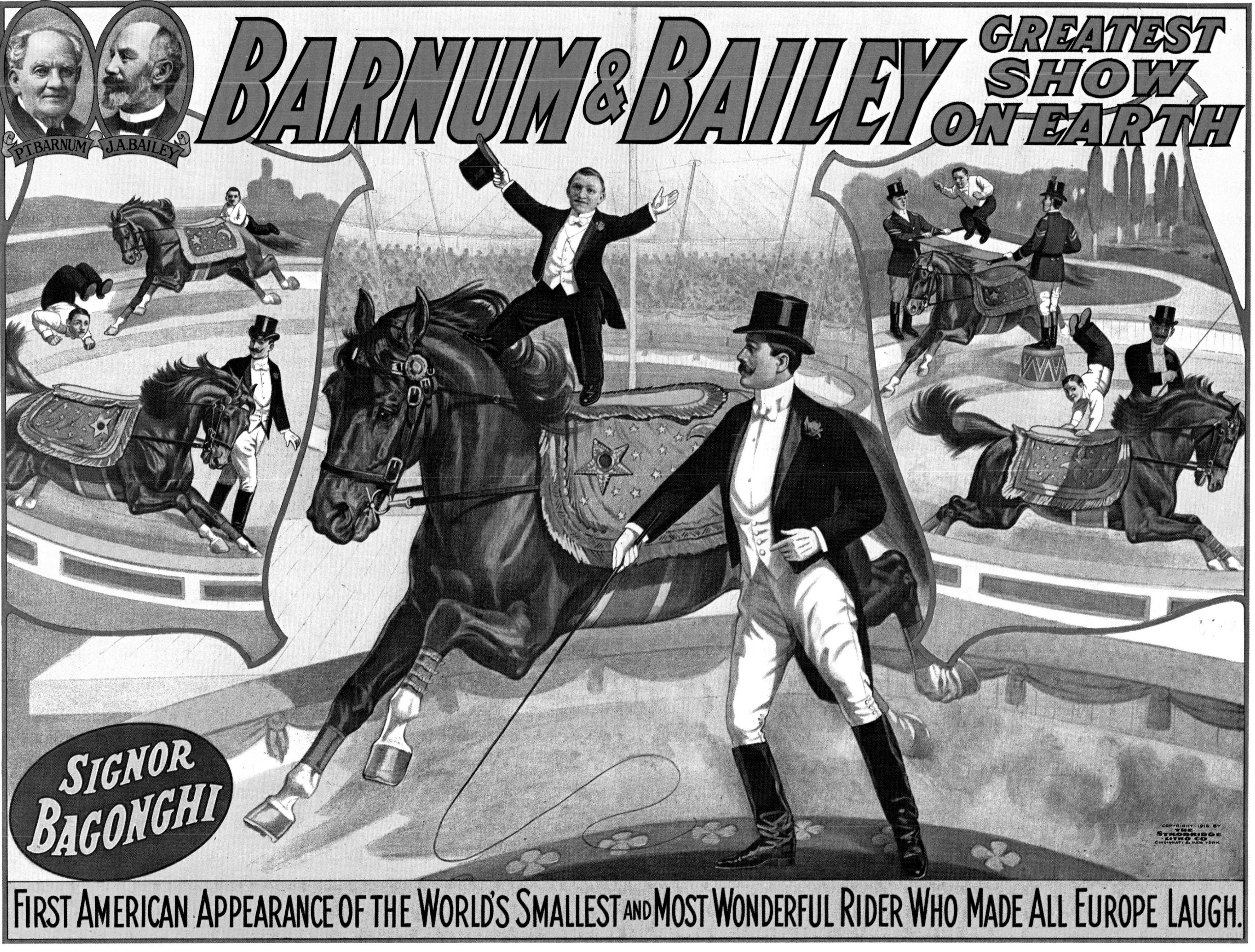

P.T. BARNUM
J.A. BAILEY
BARNUM & BAILEY
GREATEST SHOW ON EARTH
SIGNOR BAGONGHI
FIRST AMERICAN APPEARANCE OF THE WORLD'S SMALLEST AND MOST WONDERFUL RIDER WHO MADE ALL EUROPE LAUGH.

THE BARNUM & BAILEY
GREATEST SHOW ON EARTH
P.T. BARNUM
J.A. BAILEY
THE CHING-LING-HE AND TIA PEN TROUPES
FIRST TIME IN AMERICA OF THE IMPERIAL CHINESE CIRCUS STARS
NEW AND STARTLING ACTS PERFORMED ON TWO STAGES AT THE SAME TIME

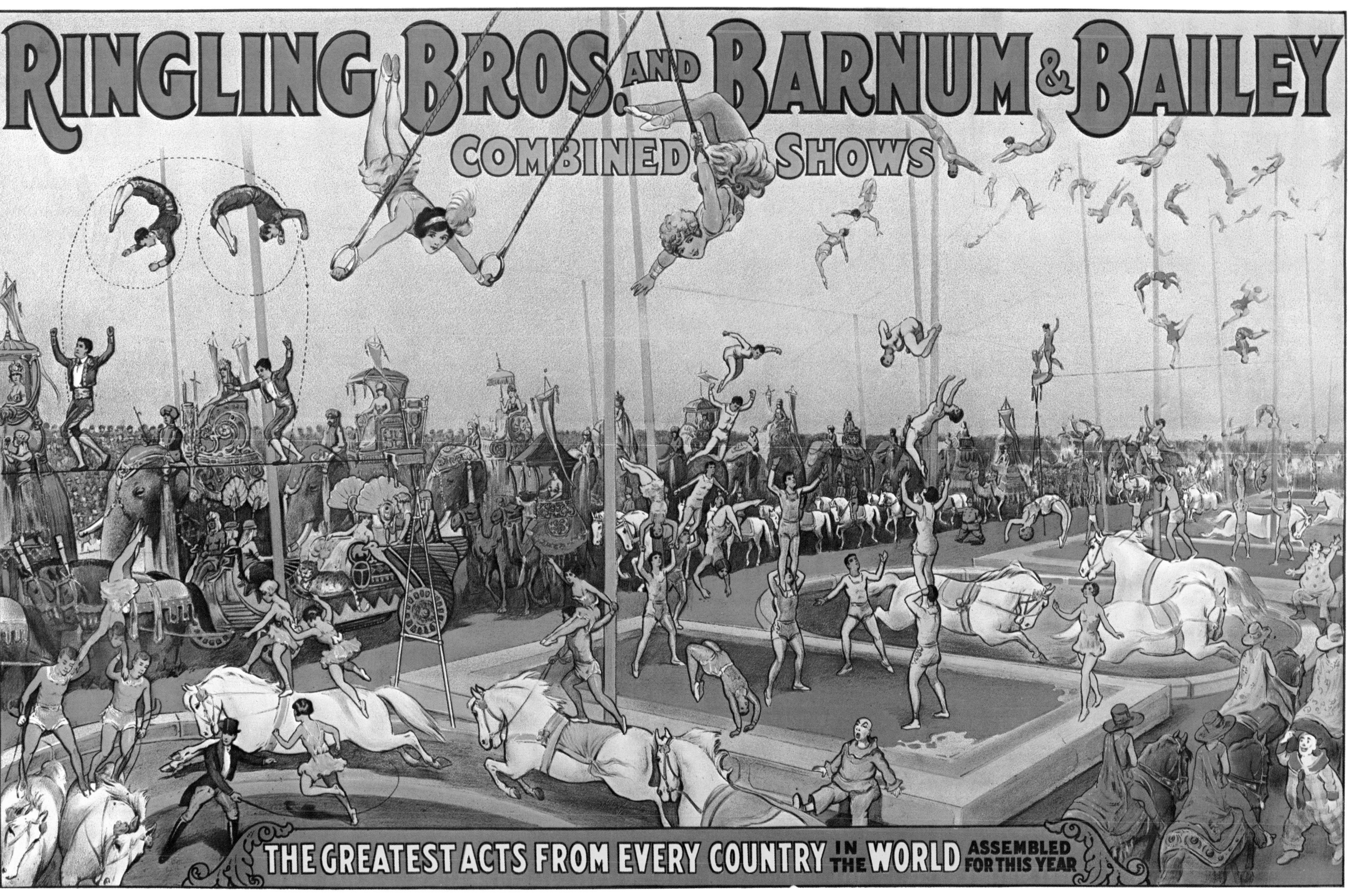
RINGLING BROS. AND BARNUM & BAILEY
COMBINED SHOWS
THE GREATEST ACTS FROM EVERY COUNTRY IN THE WORLD ASSEMBLED FOR THIS YEAR

RINGLING BROS AND
BARNUM & BAILEY
COMBINED SHOWS
WORLD FAMOUS EQUESTRIENNES
IN DARING FEATS OF HORSEMANSHIP

RINGLING BROS.
AND BARNUM & BAILEY
COMBINED SHOWS
Capt. BARRY'S FAMOUS EDUCATED EQUINES
DISPLAYING REMARKABLE INTELLIGENCE
IN ENTIRELY NEW PERFORMANCES

The Barnum & Bailey Greatest Show on Earth
ANSWERING THE ROLL CALL.
DANCING A COTILLION.
RARE ACT OF HEAD-BALANCING.
HEROIC ACT EXECUTED WITH MARVELOUS INTELLIGENCE.
CLEVER MUSICAL & DANCING TRIO.
EXCEEDINGLY CLEVER DANCING ON PEDESTALS AND BARREL ROLLING EXHIBITION.
THE STROBRIDGE LITH. CO.
A SERIES OF NEW AND MOST ASTONISHING FEATS BY THE BEST TRAINED & GREATEST HERD OF PERFORMING ELEPHANTS.
EXECUTING DIFFICULT TRICKS WITH THE EASE, GRACE, PRECISION AND CLEVERNESS OF HUMAN BEINGS.
A WONDERFUL DISPLAY OF BRUTE INTELLIGENCE AND REASON, POSITIVELY AS REPRESENTED.
THE WORLD'S GRANDEST, LARGEST, BEST, AMUSEMENT INSTITUTION.

RINGLING BROS WORLD'S GREATEST SHOWS
ALF. T.
AL.
JOHN
OTTO
CHAS.
THE COURIER LITH. CO. BUFFALO, N.Y.
THE ONLY COMPLETE & PERFECT EXPOSITION OF NATURAL HISTORY ON THIS CONTINENT.

THE ORIGINAL ADAM FOREPAUGH SHOWS.
THE STROBRIDGE LITH. Co. CIN'TI & NEW YORK
LIVING STATUES ON HORSEBACK.
BARLOW & AMPHLETT, TWO CHAMPION HORSEMEN, IN DARING ILLUSTRATIONS OF CELEBRATED STATUES, WHILE RIDING UPON BARE-BACK HORSES.
POSITIVELY THE 31st ANNUAL TOUR OF THIS GREAT SHOW.

JUST RETURNED FROM AUSTRALIA

ROMAN HIPPODROME
3 RING CIRCUS
TWO ELEVATED STAGES,
5 CONTINENT MENAGERIE
IMPERIAL JAPANESE TROUPE

SELLS BROTHERS

COMBINED WITH
HASSAN BEN ALI'S
MOORISH CARAVAN
ARABIAN NIGHTS' ENTERTAINMENT
AND SPECTACULAR
PILGRIMAGE TO MECCA

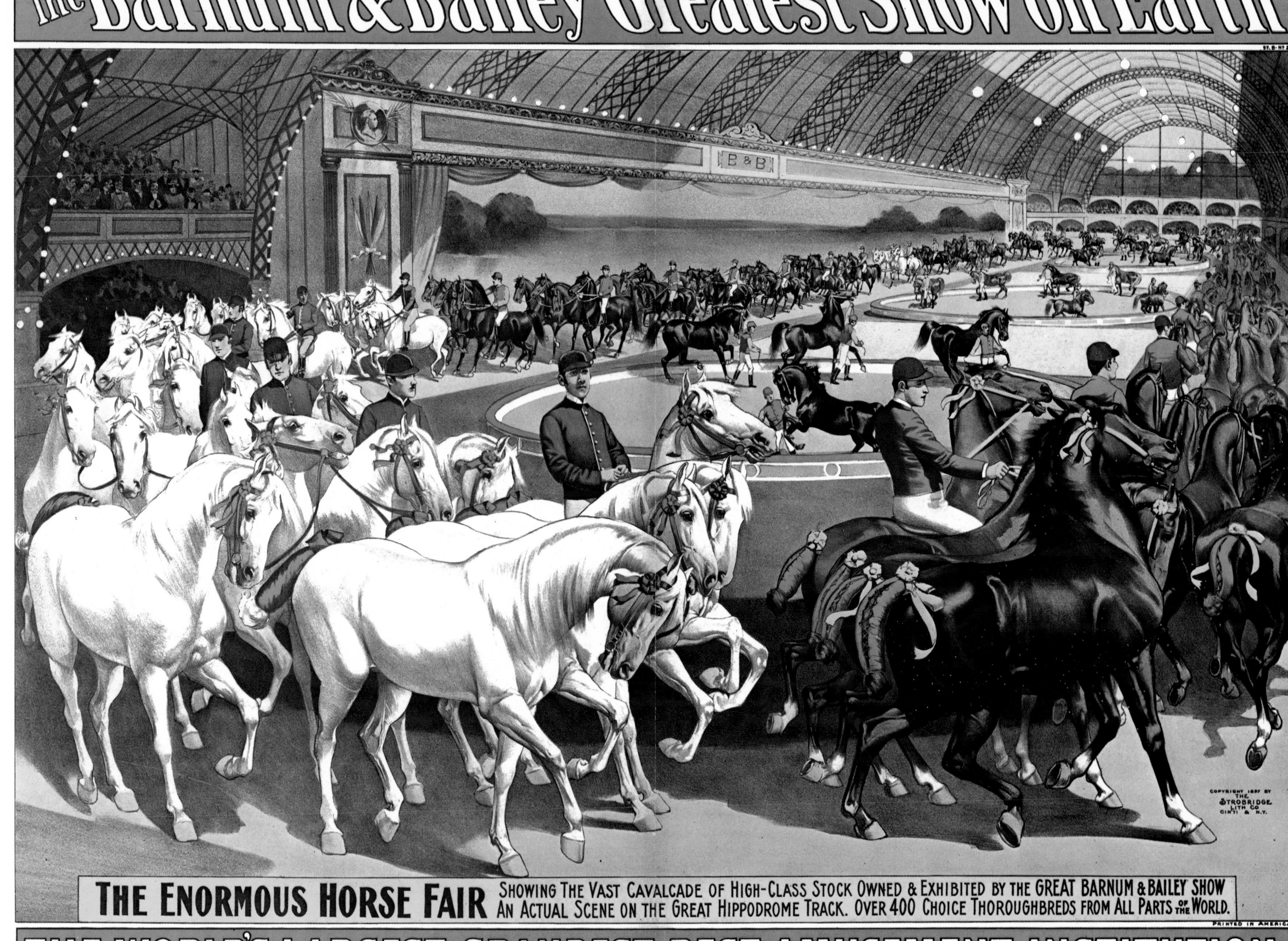
The Barnum & Bailey Greatest Show on Earth
B & B
COPYRIGHT 1897 BY THE STROBRIDGE LITH. CO. CIN'TI & N.Y.
THE ENORMOUS HORSE FAIR
SHOWING THE VAST CAVALCADE OF HIGH-CLASS STOCK OWNED & EXHIBITED BY THE GREAT BARNUM & BAILEY SHOW
AN ACTUAL SCENE ON THE GREAT HIPPODROME TRACK. OVER 400 CHOICE THOROUGHBREDS FROM ALL PARTS OF THE WORLD.
PRINTED IN AMERICA.
THE WORLD'S LARGEST, GRANDEST, BEST, AMUSEMENT INSTITUTION.

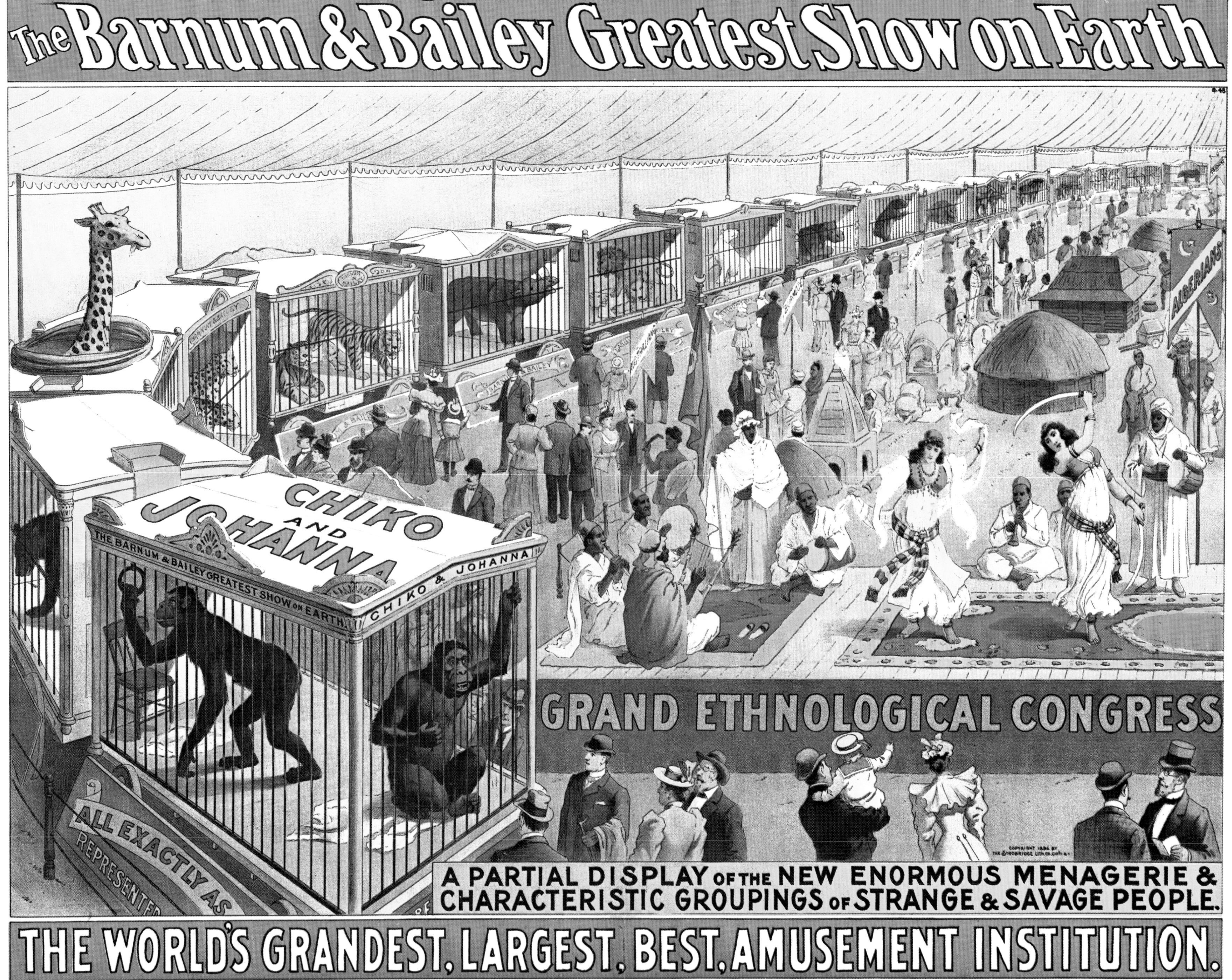
The Barnum & Bailey Greatest Show on Earth
ALGERIANS
CHIKO AND JOHANNA
THE BARNUM & BAILEY GREATEST SHOW ON EARTH
CHIKO & JOHANNA
GRAND ETHNOLOGICAL CONGRESS
ALL EXACTLY AS
REPRESENTED
A PARTIAL DISPLAY OF THE NEW ENORMOUS MENAGERIE &
CHARACTERISTIC GROUPINGS OF STRANGE & SAVAGE PEOPLE.
THE WORLD'S GRANDEST, LARGEST, BEST, AMUSEMENT INSTITUTION.

THE BARNUM & BAILEY
SUPREME PAGEANT
ALADDIN
AND HIS WONDERFUL LAMP
COPYRIGHT 1917 BY THE STROBRIDGE LITHO. CO. CINCINNATI & NEW YORK

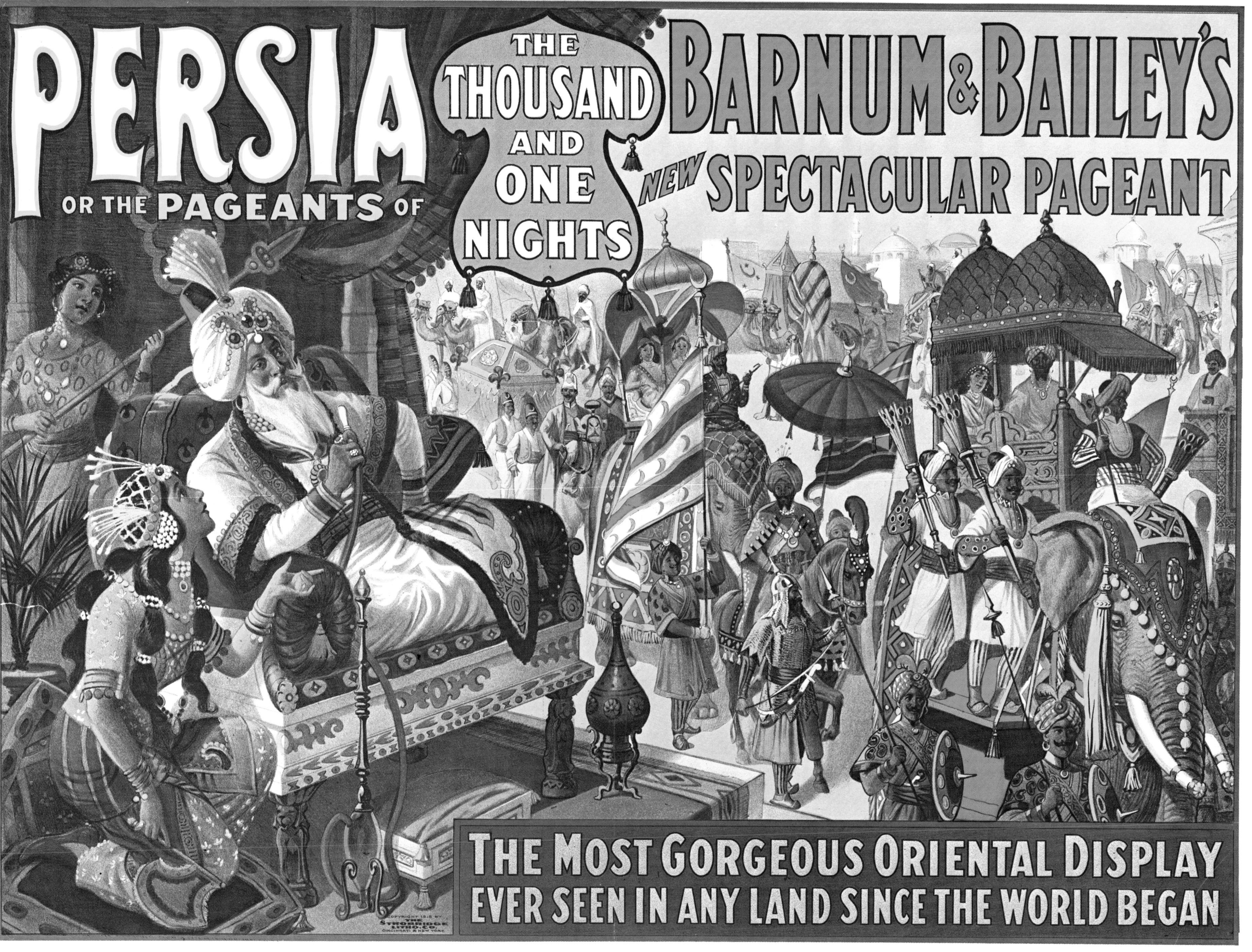
PERSIA
OR THE PAGEANTS OF
THE THOUSAND AND ONE NIGHTS
BARNUM & BAILEY'S
NEW SPECTACULAR PAGEANT
THE MOST GORGEOUS ORIENTAL DISPLAY
EVER SEEN IN ANY LAND SINCE THE WORLD BEGAN

381
RINGLING BROS
AND
BARNUM & BAILEY
COMBINED SHOWS
THE
WORLD'S
MOST
TERRIFYING
LIVING
CREATURE!
GARGANTUA
THE
GREAT
THE LARGEST AND FIERCEST
GORILLA EVER BROUGHT BEFORE
THE EYES OF CIVILIZED MAN!
LITHO. IN U.S.A.

17. B. 195
BARNUM
& BAILEY
GREATEST
SHOW ON EARTH
COPYRIGHT 1917 BY
THE
STROBRIDGE
LITHO. CO.
CINCINNATI & NEW YORK
EXCLUSIVE RARE ZOOLOGICAL FEATURES

The Barnum & Bailey Greatest Show on Earth
JOAN OF ARC
JOAN
BATTLE FOR THE STANDARD
WASHINGTON
COPYRIGHT 1903 BY THE STROBRIDGE LITHO. CO. CINCINNATI & NEW YORK
A COMPLETE HORSE SHOW OF THE MOST BEAUTIFUL, BEST TRAINED AND SAGACIOUS EQUINES EVER EXHIBITED.
AN IDEAL PRODUCTION OF ENTIRELY NEW FEATS, TRICKS, STATUESQUE ACTS AND PERFORMANCES.
THE WORLD'S LARGEST, GRANDEST, BEST, AMUSEMENT INSTITUTION.

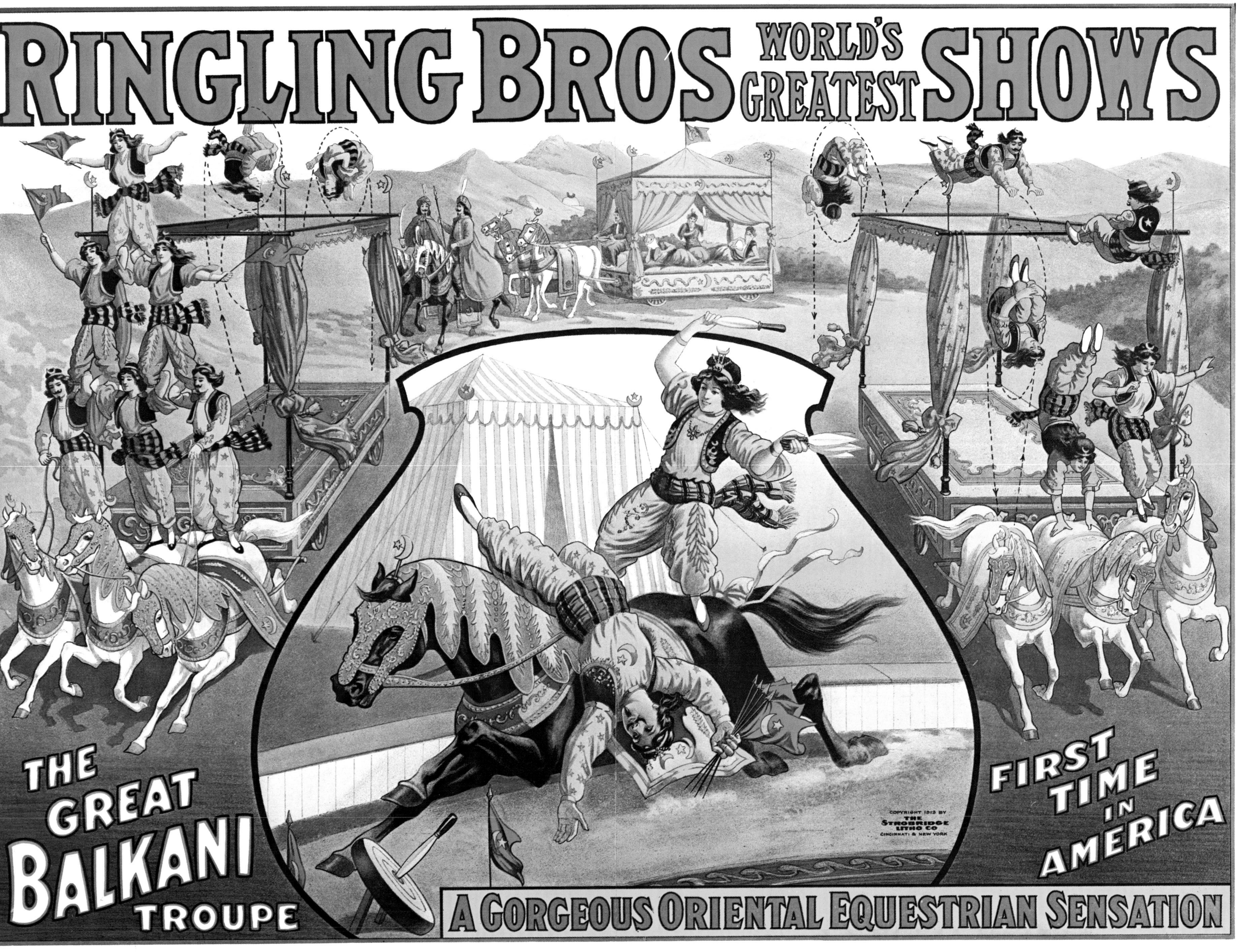
13.R-196
RINGLING BROS WORLD'S GREATEST SHOWS
THE GREAT BALKANI TROUPE
FIRST TIME IN AMERICA
COPYRIGHT 1913 BY THE STROBRIDGE LITHO CO CINCINNATI & NEW YORK
A GORGEOUS ORIENTAL EQUESTRIAN SENSATION

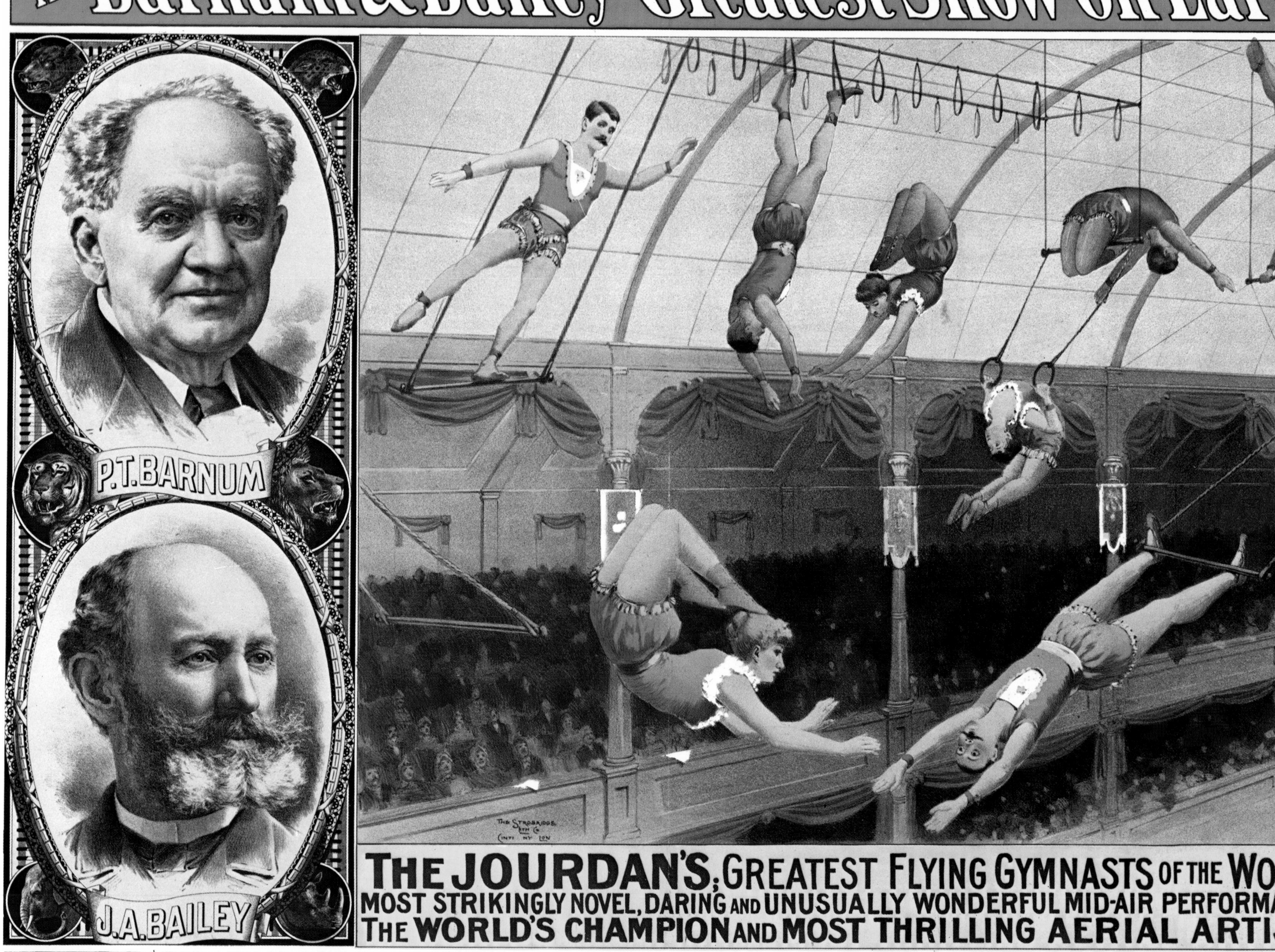
The Barnum & Bailey Greatest Show on Earth
P.T. BARNUM
J.A. BAILEY
THE JOURDAN'S; GREATEST FLYING GYMNASTS OF THE WORLD.
MOST STRIKINGLY NOVEL, DARING AND UNUSUALLY WONDERFUL MID-AIR PERFORMANCES.
THE WORLD'S CHAMPION AND MOST THRILLING AERIAL ARTISTS.
THE WORLD'S GRANDEST, LARGEST, BEST, AMUSEMENT INSTITUTION.

The Barnum & Bailey Greatest Show on Earth
B-20
THE STROBRIDGE LITH-CO.
CIN'TI - NY - LONDON
THE THREE FAMOUS HERBERT BROTHERS. ABSOLUTELY THE CHAMPIONS IN THEIR SPLENDID AND ORIGINAL LINE OF ACROBATIC PERFORMANCES.
EXECUTING WITH MARVELOUS GRACE, EASE AND PERFECTION
THE MOST EXTRAORDINARY AND INTRICATE FEATS, ON A RAISED PLATFORM.
THE WORLD'S GRANDEST, LARGEST, BEST, AMUSEMENT INSTITUTION.

The Barnum & Bailey Greatest Show on Earth
B-No 52
THE FELINE MARVELS
WONDERFUL TRAINED CATS
THE STROBRIDGE LITH. Co. CIN'TI, N.Y. LONDON
MOST WONDERFUL ADDITION TO THE CHILDREN'S CIRCUS. AN EXACT ILLUSTRATION OF THE MARVELOUS PERFORMANCES OF THE TROUPE OF TRAINED CATS AND PIGS, WHOSE CLEVER AND REMARKABLE ACTS AMAZE AND ASTOUND ALL BEHOLDERS. ACTUALLY EXECUTING A SUCCESSION OF HITHERTO IMAGINED IMPOSSIBLE FEATS.
THE WORLD'S GRANDEST, LARGEST, BEST, AMUSEMENT INSTITUTION.

THE ORIGINAL ADAM FOREPAUGH SHOWS.
THE OLDEST, LARGEST AND BEST CIRCUS AND MENAGERIE IN AMERICA
UNO. QUEEN SUPREME OF THE SERPENT KINGDOM,
ABSOLUTE MISTRESS OF THE WRITHING, STRANGLING MONSTERS.
POSITIVELY THE 31st ANNUAL TOUR OF THIS GREAT SHOW.

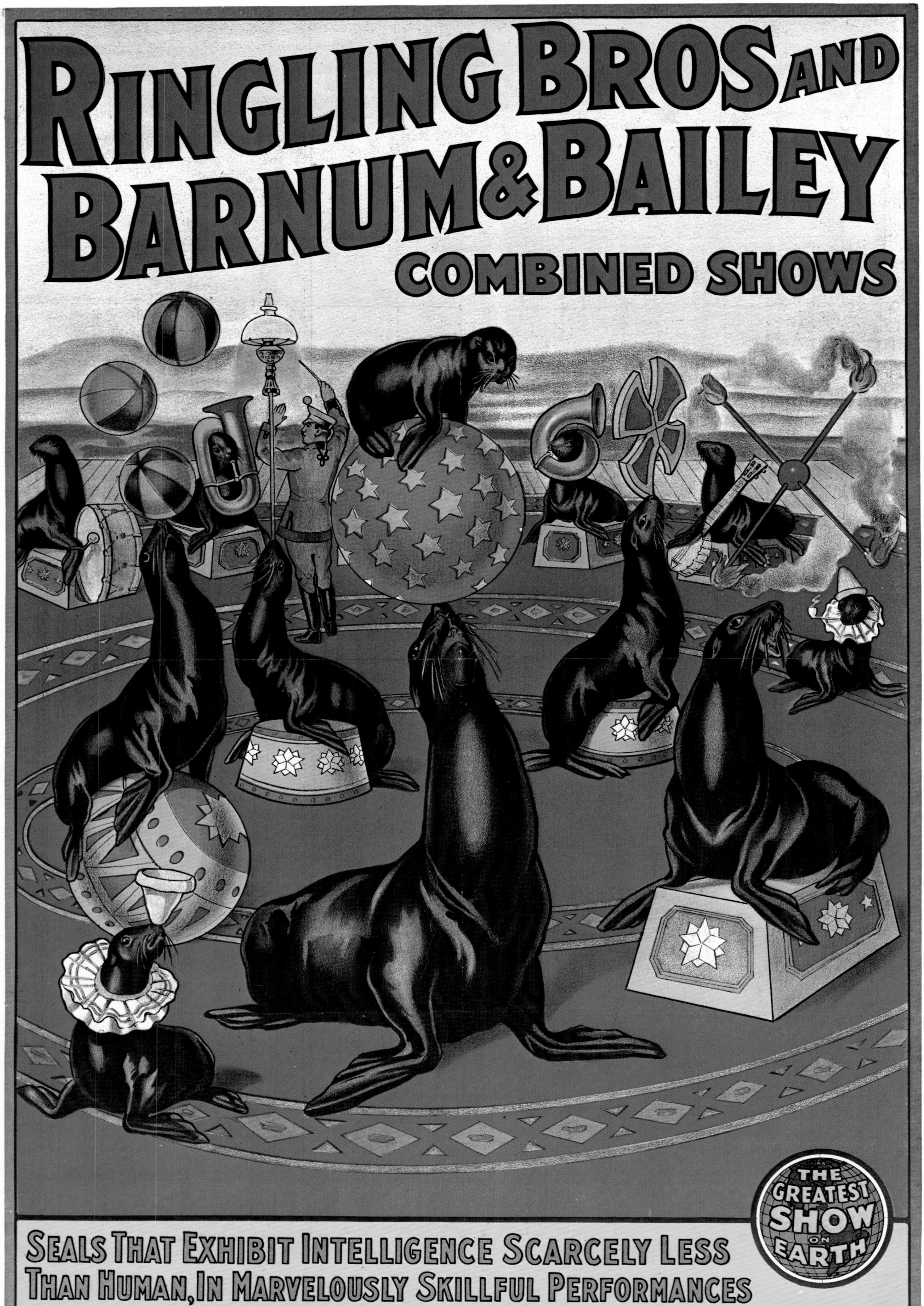
RINGLING BROS AND
BARNUM & BAILEY
COMBINED SHOWS
SEALS THAT EXHIBIT INTELLIGENCE SCARCELY LESS
THAN HUMAN, IN MARVELOUSLY SKILLFUL PERFORMANCES
THE GREATEST SHOW ON EARTH

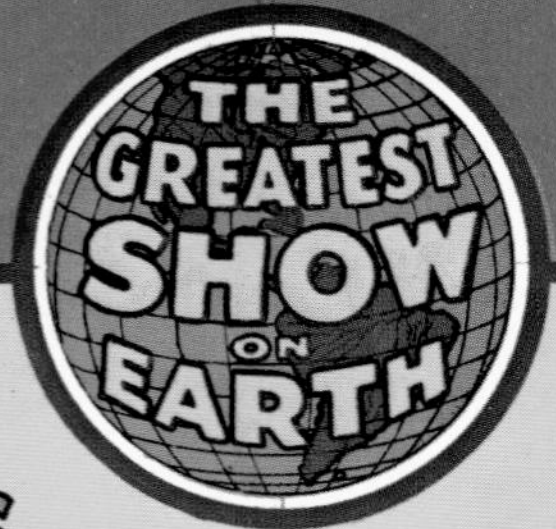

RINGLING BROS
AND
BARNUM & BAILEY
COMBINED
CIRCUS

JUST RETURNED FROM AUSTRALIA
ROMAN HIPPODROME
3 RING CIRCUS
TWO ELEVATED STAGES,
5 CONTINENT MENAGERIE
IMPERIAL JAPANESE TROUPE
SELLS BROTHERS
COMBINED WITH
HASSAN BEN ALI'S
MOORISH CARAVAN
ARABIAN NIGHTS' ENTERTAINMENT
AND SPECTACULAR
PILGRIMAGE TO MECCA
20 YEARS BEFORE THE PUBLIC.
THE SUPREME TEST OF MERIT IS SUCCESS.
BILLY CARROLL & BROTHER
ELECTRIC DUDES.
"ROMEO & JULIET"
"HERE WE GO!"
"HOW COMES THIS 'BIZNESS ANYHOW!"
"DON'T BE AFRAID! I'M HERE!"
"ME AND BROTHER BILL"
"KEEP STILL I'VE GOT HIM!"
THE CLOWNS' FROLICS, EXEMPLIFIED BY Mr. BILLY CARROLL & HIS FAMOUS FUNNY BROTHER. INTRODUCING NEW AND IMMENSELY FUNNY BUSINESS, TRANSFORMATIONS, TRICKS, SONGS AND DIALOGUES.– THIS FEATURE OF THE UNITED SHOWS SURPASSES ANYTHING EVER BEFORE SEEN WITH A CIRCUS.